Old Bathgate

Sybil Cavanagh

This lovely rural view shows Balbardie Mains Farm, the home farm of Balbardie mansion house; and behind it, the Glenmavis Distillery which takes its name from the pretty Glen Mavis that runs up the hill behind it. The earliest known tenant of the distillery was David Simpson who held the lease from 1795 to 1825 (and married the daughter of the Balbardie Mains farmer), but is better known as the father of James Young Simpson. In 1834 the distillery was taken over by John MacNab and continued to be run by him, his son and his grandson (both also John MacNab) until its demise in 1910. 'Glenmavis' wrote a visitor in 1887, 'is a picturesque and delightfully old-fashioned Distillery… The establishment is built in three sections, the central and principal range being the Still House, Mill, Mash House and Tun Room, all built on the slope of the hill… The whisky, which is pure Malt, is principally sold in Scotland and England, and shipped to many parts of the Colonies. The annual output is 80,000 gallons'.

© Sybil Cavanagh
First Published in the United Kingdom, 2006
Stenlake Publishing Limited
54–58 Mill Square
Catrine
KA5 6RD
www.stenlake.co.uk

ISBN 978-1-84033-377-0

This is Balbardie House, the home of Alexander Marjoribanks, 'the good old laird'. Alexander Marjoribanks inherited Balbardie estate when aged just sixteen. He spent over twenty years putting the estate into order, improving the land, and paying off debts. At the age of forty he married and, despite his late start, he had at least seventeen children. In the 1790s he commissioned the renowned Scottish architect, Robert Adam, to design a new mansion house. The plans were signed by Adam just three weeks before he died, so Balbardie may well have been the last house he ever designed. The house was completed in 1796 and faced north, looking over the policies and a small loch (drained in 1853). The story is a myth that the house was built the wrong way round and that the architect committed suicide. In 1805 Marjoribanks purchased the estate of Bathgate and the town has two reasons to be grateful to him. He allowed the town to be erected into a 'free and independent burgh' with its own town council in 1824. He also fought the legal battle and bore the financial risk to retain John Newland's legacy for the building of Bathgate Academy.

INTRODUCTION

The name, Bathgate, is an ancient one, and means boar wood. Early place names give a clue to the landscape in former times and the high number of Bog, Inch (island in a marsh), Moss and Muir place names in the area suggests that the early landscape of the Bathgate area was wet and marshy as well as wooded.

The early records of Bathgate are sketchy and difficult to piece together. About the year 1160, Uchtred, Sheriff of Linlithgow, and Geoffrey de Melville, at the command of King Malcolm IV, came to Bathgate and measured out an area of land, the basis of Bathgate parish. The church and its lands were granted to Holyrood Abbey, meaning that the teinds (a tenth of the produce of the land) were given to the Abbey. At some date before 1500 the church lands of Bathgate were transferred to Newbattle Abbey, a Cistercian foundation, whose monks lived very much in the community and who may have been the first to exploit the coal reserves of the Bathgate area. At the Reformation in 1560 the church lands of Bathgate passed into the hands of a former abbot, later the Earl of Lothian. Such was the shortage of reformed clergy that it was a monk of Paisley, John Hamilton, who became vicar of Bathgate in 1567. He later became a minister of the reformed Church and served in Bathgate until 1582.

In the late thirteenth century, Bathgate was in the possession of Erik, King of Norway; it was one of several estates that came to him as part of the dowry of his wife Margaret, daughter of Alexander III. In 1292, he petitioned the Scottish Parliament for arrears of rent from Bathgate and his other Scottish lands. In 1315, during the Wars of Independence, Robert the Bruce granted the barony of Bathgate to Walter the High Steward of Scotland upon his marriage to Bruce's daughter, Marjory. The young couple may have acquired an existing castle, or may have built the Castle of Bathgate. Walter the Steward died there in 1328 and was buried in Paisley Abbey. His and Marjory's son, Robert II, was the first of the Stewart dynasty of monarchs that reigned for some 500 years. Nothing now remains of Bathgate Castle (which would have been built of wood, not stone); its circular ditches form some of the natural hazards on Bathgate golf course but they can best be seen in aerial photographs.

In 1335 the Bathgate estate was split up and sold off as six smaller estates (Bathgate, Ballencrieff, Balbardie, Boghall, Barbauchlaw and Boghead). Several of them came into the hands of branches of the Hamilton family and the Hamiltons remained influential in the Bathgate area until the seventeenth century. Why the village of Bathgate was established so far from the castle and the parish church is not clear, but it may have been because the new site was less marshy than the old, and so was healthier, drier and more suited for building. In 1663 the Hamiltons gave encouragement to its growth by obtaining from the Crown a charter erecting it into a burgh of barony. Burghs of barony did not have the right to self-government through town councils, as had royal burghs like Linlithgow, but were administered by the superior through his baron bailie and the baron bailie's court. Customs paid on goods sold at the markets went not to the people of Bathgate, but to the superior. The only benefit Bathgate received was ratification of its right to hold a weekly market and seven annual fairs on the Burgh Muir.

The Earls of Hopetoun acquired the barony of Bathgate from the Hamiltons and held it until 1805 when Bathgate was sold to Alexander Marjoribanks of Balbardie, its best-remembered laird and its first provost. As superior of Bathgate, Marjoribanks had the right to grant feus, exact feu duty, hold a baron bailie court for minor offences and disputes, imprison offenders in Bathgate's jail and exact customs duties on every article sold in the town. He had no obligation to do anything for the town in the way of improvements, so little was done. In 1824 a number of Bathgate's prominent citizens applied for and were granted a private Act of Parliament to erect the town into a 'free and independent burgh of barony'. From this time onwards, the residents of Bathgate (at least the wealthier among them) ran their own affairs through the Town Council, without interference from the local laird and they had the right to levy rates for town improvements such as a decent water supply and street cleansing.

In the seventeenth and eighteenth centuries, Bathgate was a village market centre for the south of the county of West Lothian and depended on agriculture, a little coal mining, and a great deal of handloom weaving for employment. The earliest known reference to coal mining is a document of 1675 in which Thomas Hamilton, owner of the barony of Bathgate, petitioned the Lords of Exchequer to be released from confinement for debt, on the grounds that he had 'nothing for his lyvelihood and the mantenance of him and his family bot ane coall upon the lands of Bathgate... and which coall is now drowned with water by the neglect of the colziars [colliers] and servants and will altogether perish unless personall freedome wer allowed the petitioner for sieing the same dryed up...' The whereabouts of this early pit is not known, but may be one of those which over the years have caused problems of subsidence in the town centre.

By the time of the Old Statistical Account of the 1790s, Bathgate was economically dependent on handloom weaving. The weavers were prosperous then, highly paid and with plenty of leisure hours for reading and politics. Between the Old and the New Statistical Accounts (1790 to 1843) the population of Bathgate doubled – from c1,400 to 2,809, and the number of weavers in the town rose to 386 (about 40% of households). But the introduction of power loom weaving in the early nineteenth century meant a drastic drop in wages and Bathgate's weavers endured repeated periods of distress and destitution, relieved only by Council 'job creation' schemes of stone-breaking and road bottoming. The number of weavers in Bathgate reached a peak in 1851, but thereafter declined rapidly, until only seven remained by 1891.

The bequest by John Newland for the building of a school for the 'poor bairns of Bathgate' led, after a protracted legal wrangle, to the building of Bathgate Academy.

The provision of free education in a handsome school building enabled Bathgate to send out a stream of well-educated youngsters into the world. The most famous of Bathgate bairns is James Young Simpson (born too soon to benefit from the Academy), the discoverer of the anaesthetic qualities of chloroform. In the twentieth century, Bathgate golfers Eric Brown and Bernard Gallacher achieved fame and Bathgate Golf Club is the only club ever to produce two Ryder Cup captains.

1850 marks a watershed in the history of Bathgate - the railway had come to town the year before, opening up opportunities for trade and industry and making possible the heavy industries which dominated the town for the next century and more. It was fortunate for the starving weavers of Bathgate that alternative employment became available - on the railways, in the coal mines, in the flint glass works in Chapel Lane (Mansefield Street) and in the foundries and shovel works. Bathgate became a town of heavy engineering - bustling, smoky and soot-covered - the shopping and commercial focus for the south of the county. Because of its rapid expansion, house-building never caught up with population growth and bad housing was the single biggest problem facing Bathgate for the century after 1850. In 1901 two thirds of the population lived in one or two rooms and West Lothian as a whole was the worst housed county in Scotland. Bathgate's housing problem was not solved until the council house building programme of 1919-1975, in the course of which over three thousand homes were built. By 1971 such was the preponderance of council housing that only 16% of householders were owner-occupiers. However, after a huge amount of private house building and council house sales, this proportion has risen to nearly 60%.

Coal mining became important from 1850, when James (Paraffin) Young set up his chemical works at Boghead to extract oil from the Torbanite coal of the Boghead mines. This was probably the first commercial oil works in the world and it started the shale oil industry that was so important to West Lothian for the next 110 years. Balbardie Collieries in the grounds of Balbardie House came into operation in the 1850s, despoiling the once sylvan policies and begriming the mansion house. In 1898 Easton Colliery came into operation and was the longest surviving and most successful of Bathgate's coal mines. By 1901 the population of the town had swollen to over 6,786, at which time over 800 Bathgate men were employed in coal mining. If it had been suggested to these men that within 80 years, the industry would have disappeared from Bathgate, they would been incredulous. Yet Boghead closed in the 1920s, Balbardie became a training pit and escape shaft for Easton, and Easton itself, the second last deep mine in West Lothian, closed down in 1973.

After the Second World War, the government, aware that heavy industry was in terminal decline, undertook to disperse some of the nationalised industries to the assisted areas. The British Motor Corporation (later British Leyland) was directed to build its new truck and tractor plant at Bathgate. Thousands of new houses had to be built to accommodate a workforce of 6,000 at its peak and, at the same time, several hundred Glasgow overspill families.

Mismanagement, reluctance to stay in Scotland, foreign competition and poor industrial relations combined to bring about the closure of British Leyland in 1986, a period of deep economic depression when every week brought news of more job losses and closures. Salvation was thought to lie in the hi-tech electronic industries, but Motorola and NEC in turn have come and gone. Regeneration has come through the re-opening of the Bathgate-Edinburgh railway line, which has encouraged Bathgate's growth as a commuter town with easy links to both Edinburgh and Glasgow. Bathgate has benefited from the jobs available in Livingston, but also suffered from its proximity. The New Town has attracted most of the new (and some of the existing) industries, institutions and shops, at the expense of all the older surrounding communities – at least that is the perception of many Bathgate residents. Despite this, the population today is 15,544 – and rising.

In the local government reorganisation of 1975 the burgh of Bathgate became part of West Lothian District. Bathgate Town Council was abolished, bringing to an end 150 years of burgh independence.

Further Reading

The Statistical Account of Scotland, Vol.II – The Lothians 1790s Reprinted by E. P. Publishing Ltd, 1973
The New Statistical Account of Scotland -- Linlithgowshire William Blackwood & Sons, 1845
The Third Statistical Account of Scotland, County of West Lothian Edited by Patrick Cadell Scottish Academic Press, 1992
Bisset, Alexander M. *History of Bathgate and District* West Lothian Printing and Publishing Company,1906
Borrowman, Stuart. *Silicon Glen – West Lothian: transformed for good* Drumduff Publications, 2000
Hendrie, William F. *Bathgate - Images of Scotland Series* Tempus Publishing Ltd, 2001
Hendrie, William F & Mackie, Allister. (ed.s) *The Bathgate Book: a History of Bathgate* Bathgate 2000 Trust, 2001
The West Lothian Courier, 1873 to date

These tall and handsome houses in Cochrane Street are a reminder that Cochrane Street was once one of the most important streets in Bathgate. The old main road between Edinburgh and Glasgow came into the town along here, up Main Street and through Gideon Street onto Drumcross Hill, then out along the old Bangour road. Cochrane Street was named after Alexander Cochrane of Barbauchlaw, a sheriff of Bathgate in the late seventeenth century (when some of these houses were built). In the distance can be seen part of North Street. It was described in the Ordnance Survey name books of the 1850s as 'a narrow crooked street or lane extending from Kaim Head to Brown's Square; the houses are chiefly one storey high, having a dead wall in front, and occupied by weavers and labourers. There are vegetable gardens in rear of the houses on the north side, Cochrane Street was re-built with council houses in the 1930s, and North Street was demolished in the redevelopment of Bathgate in the 1960s.

The pantiled white cottage is the toll house at Guildiehaugh. Invisible in the trees behind is Kaim Park, a Victorian villa, now a hotel. The tollhouse was built in the 1790s, when the new road between Edinburgh and Glasgow opened – the Bathgate-Airdrie route. It was a turnpike road, built by the local landowners who formed themselves into a turnpike trust and raised money to build and maintain the new road on the security of future tolls. Every six miles or so, there was a tollhouse where a gate barred the way to all but pedestrians. Travellers in wheeled vehicles, or with herds of animals paid a toll - a sliding scale of charges according to the size and weight of their cart or carriage or the number of animals – then the gate was opened and they would go on their way. Many toll-keepers were also licensed to sell ale and spirits to travellers – no scruples in those days about drinking and driving! Tolls were abolished by law in 1878 and the Guildiehaugh tollhouse was knocked down in 1910, but Guildiehaugh is still referred to simply as 'The Toll' by Bathgate Bairns.

Ballencrieff Toll, Bathgate.

Ballencrieff Toll (the pantiled cottage on the right) was a tollhouse on the Cleugh Turnpike road, which was built in 1781 to bring iron from the early ironworks at Wilsontown through West Lothian to the harbour at Bo'ness. The road crossed the Breich Water at the Breich Inns, came north via East Whitburn and the old bridge at Stepends, through Bathgate and out by the High Street to Torphichen, Linlithgow and Bo'ness. The minutes of the Cleugh Turnpike Trust survive in the West Lothian Local History Library and make interesting reading. At the roup (auction) of tolls in 1800, John Marshall offered forty-five pounds sterling for the right to levy the tolls at Ballencrieff for a year. The forty-five pounds were used by the trustees to maintain the road, while John Marshall got to keep all the tolls paid at his tollbar. The scale of tolls was fixed by the trustees, varying from two shillings for a coach and six horses, down to a penny for a saddle horse and seven pence halfpenny per score of cattle in a cattle drove.

Older residents may still remember the Kirkton Kilns that stood where Marina Road joins Puir Wife's Brae. There were two kilns, which were supplied with lime from the quarry at nearby Limefield Farm. When builders in Edinburgh New Town and agricultural improvers began to seek huge quantities of lime in the eighteenth century, Bathgate was well-placed to provide it, with quarries and limekilns at Ballencrieff Toll, Petershill, Gateshiels, South Mains and Kirkton. In the nineteenth century, however, the coming of the railways meant that lime production could be concentrated in large works, rather than at isolated rural kilns. Most kilns ceased to operate after the middle of the nineteenth century. At the time of the New Statistical Account (1843), Bathgate's minister, the Rev. Samuel Martin, wrote that the Kirkton limeworks had recently been suspended. The Kirkton kilns, though unused, survived until 1967, when they were demolished to make way for housing in the Boghall scheme.

If on leaving Bathgate by the Torphichen road, you were to take the first right turn at Ballencrieff Toll, you would go up this road to Sunnyside Reservoir, with Gateshiels Farm by the roadside in the distance. You might also catch a glimpse of the Gateshiels limekilns, now in the garden of a private house. Gateshiels was part of the estate of Balbardie, the property of the Marjoribanks family. From the mid eighteenth century, lime was quaried on the Gateshiels land and burned in kilns - egg shaped and brick lined and built into a stone-faced structure. The limestone was put into the kilns through an opening at the top and layered with coal. It then burned for hours, and the lime was raked out through the arched doorways at the foot. In 1827 ten men and four horses were employed at Gateshiels kilns, producing 7,000 bolls of lime each year. The kilns ceased to operate in the 1880s.

The history of Academy Street is a reminder of Bathgate's century as a centre of handloom weaving (c.1750-1850). Bathgate's economy depended on weaving, and at its height in 1851, there were 476 weavers and ancillary workers in the town. The industry went into terminal decline from the 1820s because of the introduction of steam powered looms: wages fell and the work dried up. Once the educated elite of Bathgate, known for their radical politics, the weavers faced destitution and made repeated appeals for assistance to Bathgate Town Council during the 1820s, 1830s and 1840s. In 1825 the Council agreed to employ some of the 300 unemployed weavers in building a new road from Mid Street to the Edinburgh Road. The work was later extended to join up with Marjoribanks Street at the Academy, thus creating Academy Street. Academy Street was sometimes referred to as Radical Road, because it was built by the radical weavers.

This handsome building was built on the proceeds of slavery. John Newland was a Bathgate bairn who went to Jamaica and acquired a sugar plantation. At his death in 1799 he had no (legitimate) offspring, so he left his estate (including slaves named Thomas, Bob, Cufee, James, Nera, Caesar and Sampson) to be disposed of and the funds invested to build 'a free school in such parts of the said parish of Bathgate'. The will was contested by his sister Margaret and, after a protracted lawsuit, only about a quarter of the intended sum came to Bathgate. It was invested for another 15 years; then at last, in 1833, the school was opened. The Academy had a fine record of academic achievement and continued to educate the youth of Bathgate and the south-west part of West Lothian until the new Academy came into use in 1967. The slope of the playground added interest to games of tennis on the courts in front of the school. John Newland is remembered in the annual Procession which begins at the old Academy and will continue to do so although the school has now been converted into flats. The oration, however, now takes place at the High Church.

Hill Street (or The Hill) was one of the most interesting streets in old Bathgate. Here (nearest on the right) was the house in which John Newland was born. The Newland's Day procession always stopped here and laid a wreath in his honour. At the top of Hill Street was the old market place, at first just an open space, but later with enclosed buildings for the different produce – the fleshmarket, the mealmarket and, at the foot of The Hill, the butter market. In the market place was the mercat cross, the place of public proclamations and punishments. The jail, which was built in the market place about 1760, later acquired the name 'The Cross'. A new jail was built in 1828 behind the existing one. The old one, with its high walls and thick door studded with rusty iron spikes, was taken down in 1887. The 1828 jail was demolished in 1923 and its stone used for road bottoming during the widening of the Edinburgh Road between Mid Street and the Kaim Park.

Gideon Street was named after Gideon Martin, a brewer of ale and porter, who owned many of the houses in the street. His inn was on the southwest (left) side of the street, near the Hopetoun Street end and had a marriage stone above the lintel of the door bearing the initials of himself and his wife, Barbara Manners, and their marriage date of 1779. The original Masonic Lodge and the original Co-operative Buildings were in Gideon Street, but as the centre of Bathgate moved south and west towards Hopetoun Street and Engine Street, Gideon Street declined in importance. A new Masonic Lodge and new Co-operative buildings were both built in Jarvey Street. Today, practically all the old houses in Gideon Street have been demolished and even the street line of the northeast side has been lost. The Glenmavis Tavern happily still survives and is probably one of Bathgate's oldest pubs.

The changing nature of Bathgate in the mid nineteenth century is evident in this photograph – the eighteenth century weavers' houses in the foreground and the taller nineteenth century tenements of the industrial age in the distance. Groome's Ordnance Gazetteer sums up the changes: before 1850 – 'The inhabitants... had little other employment than hand-loom weaving and lived in a state of penury...'; but after the coming of heavy industry: 'Bathgate soon grew to threefold its former extent, and passed from a state of stagnancy and decay to one of bustle and prosperity...' Known in the old days as Shuttle Row because of all the handloom weavers who lived and worked there, the High Street had a social mix of residents. Weavers lived next door to professionals such as Dominie MacGregor and Thomas Dodds, the solicitor. The three Bathgate doctors - Dickson, Kirk and Longmuir – rubbed shoulders with men like the once famous John Stark ('Starkie') in his 'wee snug theekit biel – a queer auld farrant chiel'. Most of the houses in the High Street and even the route of the street were lost in the 1960s.

Markets in Bathgate were originally held in the market square at the top of The Hill. By the beginning of the nineteenth century the market site had moved to Jarvey Street and here farmers would sell their grain and other produce from their carts lined up in the street. The congestion was so great that it was decided to build an indoor market, and the Corn Exchange (in front of the tree) was opened in 1857. Over the next century and a half, the Corn Exchange served as public hall, meeting room and Council chambers. From its balcony, the Provost and Bailies would make public pronouncements or preside over celebrations and parades. By the 1950s it had become the Palais de Danse, owned by Jim and Jean McLeod and many a local couple first met and courted at the 'Pally'. Towards the end of its life the Corn Exchange was used as a nightclub and suffered the indignity of being painted black. After several years of dereliction it was demolished in 2003. Also in Jarvey Street, on the other side of the road, are the fine 1902 building of the Lodge Torphichen Kilwinning No13, the Co-op Halls (burnt down in 1996), and the Volunteer Arms, named after the Volunteers, forerunners of the Territorial Army, who were active in Bathgate from the 1860s.

In the days of horse-drawn transport, sale of the dung that was swept up thrice weekly from the town's streets brought additional income to the burgh's coffers. The 'dung depot' was located in North Bridge Street, which at that time was a mainly residential area. Not surprisingly, the residents of North Bridge Street in 1857 petitioned the council to re-locate it, because of the stench. However, it was not until 1869 that the dung depot was moved to Boghead Bridge – well away from houses. For 60 years, the town well was in Hopetoun Street, but in 1857, it was moved to the top of North Bridge Street. It was not a well sunk into the ground; it was a wellhead to which the water was brought along lead pipes. The town well was replaced by the McLagan Fountain in 1879, gifted to Bathgate by the wife of Linlithgowshire's MP, Peter McLagan of Pumpherston. When the fountain was moved to the Steelyard (where it still stands), the top of North Bridge Street became known derisively as 'the fountainless cross'.

Marjoribanks Street developed in the Victorian age as the street for Bathgate's aspiring middle class. On both sides it is lined with pleasing stone villas, including Wellpark which was well-known in Bathgate for some eighty years as education offices, police headquarters, public library and Library HQ. Alexander Marjoribanks donated a site (Rule's Acre) for the building of Bathgate Academy long before the school was built and the road was known then as College Street. As early as 1829, however, a Town Council minute refers to Marjoribanks Street, named after the man who ensured that Bathgate finally received John Newland's bequest for the building of the Academy. At the far end of the street was poorer housing where some of the last of Bathgate's weavers lived. One of those tenement buildings was nicknamed Eemoch Hill (anthill) presumably because of its teeming population. Also in Marjoribanks Street was the Chapel Well, near the site of an ancient pre-Reformation chapel. Ruins of the chapel survived into the nineteenth century, and a few years ago the well was re-discovered and has been made the focal point of an attractive little garden.

Infant School, Mid Street, Bathgate.

Until the late nineteenth century, education was the responsibility of the Church of Scotland. In 1872 the state took over and administered it through publicly elected school boards in each parish or burgh. By then the old parochial school of Bathgate was in a dilapidated state – damp, badly ventilated and the roof 'entirely worn out'. It was pulled down and a new 'board' school built (1882-83) on the same site in Mid Street. This school was known to generations of Bathgate children as 'the Wee Public', as it became Bathgate's infant school when the 'Big Public' opened in Torphichen Street in 1905. Used latterly as a post office sorting office, this old school was demolished in 1974, and a health centre (now disused) was built on the site. The lane beside the school, formerly known as the Parish School Entry, survives as a footpath between Mid Street and Marjoribanks Street.

By 1902 the old board school (in Mid Street) had become too small for the burgeoning population of the town and so the Combined School Board of Bathgate bought land at the head of the High Street, and built this fine new school. At the opening ceremony the architect (J.G. Fairley) declined to take any public part, saying that 'he would rather make ten schools and five kirks than one speech'. He was credited with having 'done so much to improve the architectural beauty of the town', being also the architect of the Dreadnought Hotel and St David's Church. The school consisted of 'eight spacious, high-roofed and well-lit classrooms, giving accommodation for 480 children, provision having been made for teaching sixty pupils in each room'. In the windows of the hall on the second storey was a 'fine series of etchings by Flaxman… of scenes from Homer's Odyssey'. After the Second World War the school became Bathgate Junior Secondary, then, after the building of the new Bathgate Academy, it became Balbardie Primary School.

The Lindsay High School (named after the Rev. John Lindsay, minister of St John's Church and first convener of the West Lothian Education Authority) opened in 1931, on the same day as St Mary's RC Academy next door. It was intended to offer vocational education to pupils not wishing to follow an academic course at Bathgate Academy and provided four types of 'technical' courses – Industrial, Rural, Commercial and Domestic. Thanks to a grant from the Miners' Welfare Committee, it even boasted a 100-yard long mine underneath the school to teach the boys mining techniques. In 1967 the government introduced the comprehensive system, putting an end to the division into Senior and Junior secondary schools. A new Bathgate Academy was built to accommodate all secondary school pupils and the Lindsay High School closed in 1967. The building became part of St Mary's RC Academy. It in turn closed down when St Margaret's Academy in Livingston opened. The buildings were demolished in 1996, and have been replaced with housing, but the old schools are commemorated in the street names, Lindsay Gardens and St Mary's Place. Strangely, the names have been transposed - Lindsay Gardens is on the site of St Mary's, and St Mary's Place on the site of the Lindsay.

Hopetoun Street was developed in the second half of the eighteenth century and was named after the Earls of Hopetoun, owners of the barony of Bathgate at that time. It still boasts some pleasant Georgian properties, notably the old Bathgate Hotel at the corner with Jarvey Street. In 1856 Hopetoun Street was the 'second best street' in the town (Jarvey Street being the best), where the town's more prosperous citizens aspired to live. The building with the distinctive curved wall was built in 1857 as the Royal Bank of Scotland, but the area was undermined. In June 1923 the Courier reported: 'In the early hours of Sabbath morning, people in the vicinity of the centre part of Hopetoun Street, Bathgate, were aroused by the sound of breaking glass. Several shop windows burst outwards, roofs collapsed, pavements rose by as much as six inches, paving stones and house walls cracked open, and gas mains burst'. The cause was the subsidence of old mine workings which lie below Hopetoun, Mid, and Jarvey Streets. This movement stabilised, but further subsidence in the 1970s caused the Council in 1977 to demolish the buildings on the south side (right) of High Hopetoun Street.

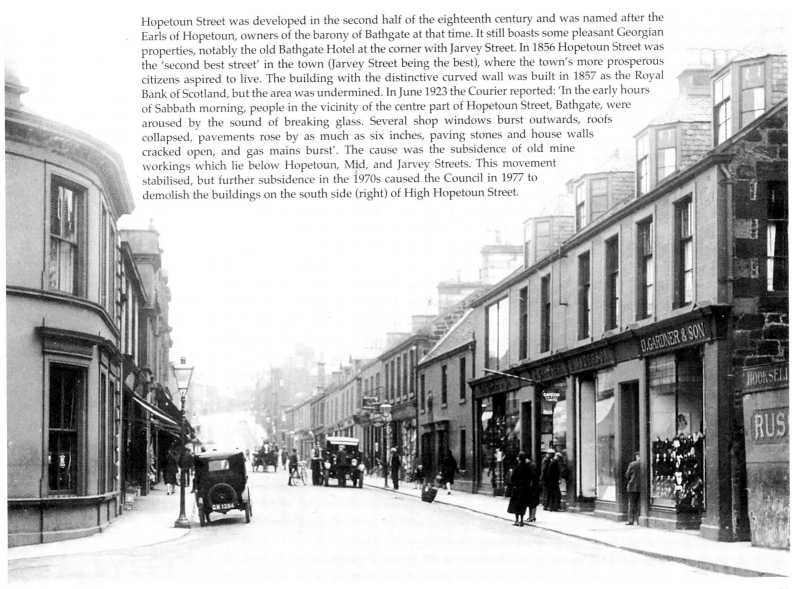

The names North and South Bridge Street refer to the bridge over the Bathgate Water, once the burgh boundary. The streets were built at the very end of the eighteenth century to join the old town of Bathgate to the new turnpike road. North Bridge Street was re-built in the late Victorian era - prosperity and confidence exude from its buildings. On the left is the Royal Bar. There has been a public house on this site at the top of Engine Street (George Street) since at least 1837. Among its best-known shops in days gone by was the Bee-Hive drapery store, founded in 1914 by Mr Reid. It passed to his son-in-law William Gibb – 'dapper Willie, keen Rotarian and churchman' who was succeeded by his son and daughter, before closing in 1971. Another well-remembered shop was Cameron's the draper's, at the corner of Livery Street. Its original owner started out with just some goods in 'an oilskin pack, peddling out the Edinburgh Road, Livingston, Starlaw, Deans, Blackburn and even Uphall. He was succeeded by his son, Herbert Cameron'. North Bridge Street remains one of Bathgate's shopping streets.

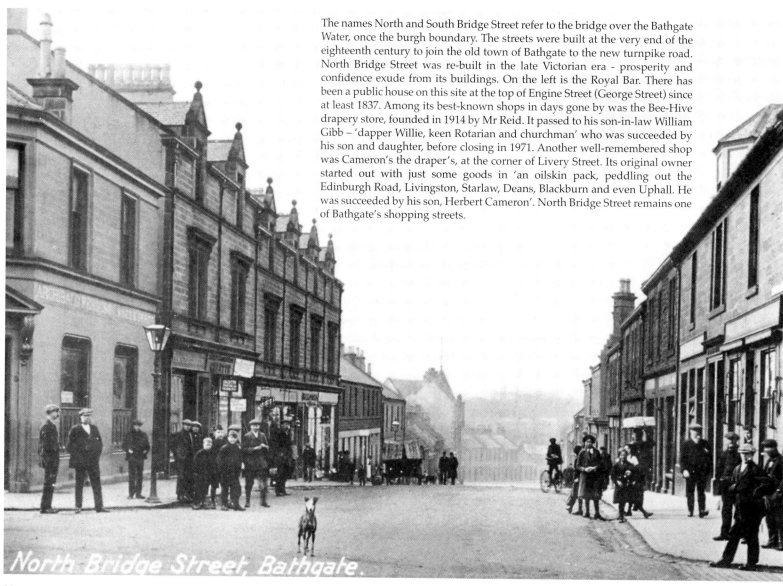

North Bridge Street, Bathgate.

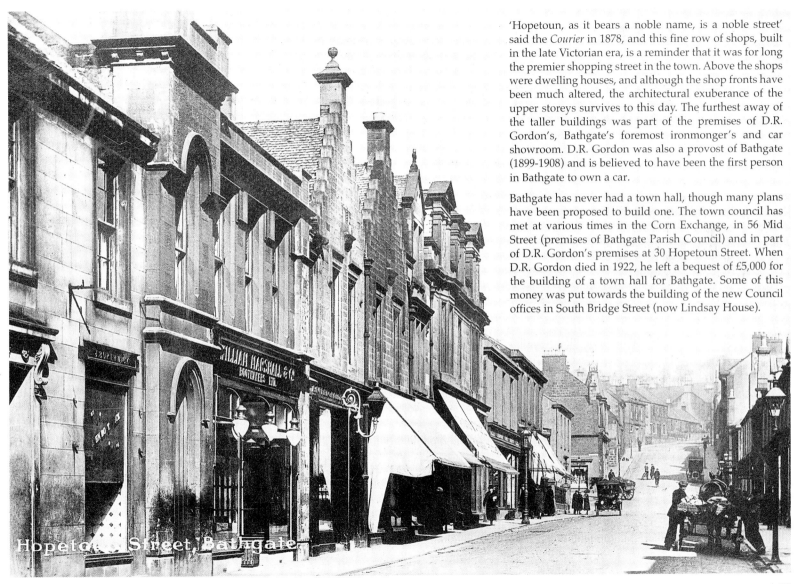

Hopetoun Street, Bathgate

'Hopetoun, as it bears a noble name, is a noble street' said the *Courier* in 1878, and this fine row of shops, built in the late Victorian era, is a reminder that it was for long the premier shopping street in the town. Above the shops were dwelling houses, and although the shop fronts have been much altered, the architectural exuberance of the upper storeys survives to this day. The furthest away of the taller buildings was part of the premises of D.R. Gordon's, Bathgate's foremost ironmonger's and car showroom. D.R. Gordon was also a provost of Bathgate (1899-1908) and is believed to have been the first person in Bathgate to own a car.

Bathgate has never had a town hall, though many plans have been proposed to build one. The town council has met at various times in the Corn Exchange, in 56 Mid Street (premises of Bathgate Parish Council) and in part of D.R. Gordon's premises at 30 Hopetoun Street. When D.R. Gordon died in 1922, he left a bequest of £5,000 for the building of a town hall for Bathgate. Some of this money was put towards the building of the new Council offices in South Bridge Street (now Lindsay House).

Bathgate butchers clad in their traditional blue and white striped aprons stand at the door of the Fleshing department of Bathgate Co-operative Society. The Co-operative movement began in Lancashire in 1844 and reached Bathgate in 1859 when a group of six men decided to set up a Co-operative Baking Society. At first bread was the only product sold, but trade was good, premises were bought in Gideon Street and, in 1863, the name Bathgate Co-operative Society was adopted. In 1903 the Co-op moved to Jarvey Street and this photograph shows part of the complex of shops, stables, stores and houses which made up 24-44 Jarvey Street (opposite the High Church) in the years before the First World War. Bathgate Co-op continued to expand: by 1938 it employed 200 people and in 1950 it had nearly 6,000 members, sharing an annual dividend of £70,000. By the 1960s and 1970s, the Co-op was facing stiff competition, particularly from self-service supermarkets. After a series of mergers, Bathgate Co-op became part of the Scottish Midland Co-op (later Scotmid). Today the Scotmid toiletries store, Semi-Chem, is the last remnant of the Co-op in Bathgate.

Bathgate was the commercial and market centre for the southern half of West Lothian, as Linlithgow was for the northern. In 1825 Pigot's Commercial Directory reported that 'Bathgate is a very healthy place, has a fine southern exposure, and is seen at a considerable distance from the west and south; the most of the streets are paved, and the houses are generally well-built and slated, and the town upon the whole has a pleasant appearance'. Even by that early date there were over forty shops in the town. The great change came after 1850, when Bathgate was transformed from a town of cottage industries into an industrial and mining centre. John Hardy's shop (nearest the camera) was a landmark in Bathgate for well over a century. The first John Hardy, a door-to-door packman, set up his first shop at the corner of Hopetoun Street and Engine Street in 1865. He prospered, and built this three-storey block a few years later. His high-class drapery shop clothed generations of Bathgate people. John Hardy the third was Provost of Bathgate from 1970 to 1973. The shop closed in 1999 and has been demolished.

Imaginatively named Mid Street is midway between the more aristocratic Marjoribanks Street and more prosaic Engine Street. It developed as part of the 'well squared off' New Town of Bathgate in the early years of the nineteenth century. On the left was M'Kill's corner, otherwise known as Bargaly House: 'Famous Bible Warehouse, Book Stores, Ironmongery Store, Clock and Silver Plate Stores'. At M'Kill's Great Shipping Bureau, 'You and your friends who intend going to Canada, United Sates, South Africa, India, should book your passages'. Robert McKill was also a Town and Parish Councillor and a School Board member, active in the Volunteers and in the YMCA, and also a fine curler. On the right of the photograph, part of the pub that was originally the Market Inn can be seen. About 1930 it was taken over by John Flannigan and bore his name for some 50 years. Its barmaid from 1933 until her death in 1971 at the age of 77 was Miss Jean Love – Scotland's oldest barmaid!

This triangular building is still a distinctive landmark in Bathgate and was another of Councillor Robert M'Kill's business ventures. At the time of his sudden death in 1909, the Courier remarked that 'he had been cut off in the midst of a large building scheme, which is nearing completion, at the junction of North and South Bridge Street, his intention having been to remove from his present quarters (in Mid Street) and centralise his large and growing business in a more prominent part of the town. His demise has cut short his ambitions, which is all the more to be regretted, as the building when completed, will be the handsomest pile in Bathgate'. Older residents will remember the ground floor being the 'Scone Shop'.

Engine Street, Bathgate

The name Engine Street is a reminder of Bathgate's coal mining past. It was the street which led to the early stationary steam engine installed south of the Edinburgh Road, to drain a coal mine of the late eighteenth century. As the centre of the town moved from the old town to the new, Engine Street grew in importance. It was one of the roads which connected Bathgate to the new turnpike road between Edinburgh and Glasgow after 1849 it was the road which led to the railway station and became one of the main shopping streets in the town. The old St David's (Bathgate United Free) Church can be glimpsed on the left beside the tree. The photograph was taken in 1903 just prior to the church's demolition in 1904.

The Steelyard and Engine Street are seen here in their heyday. On the right, beyond the Woolston Cycle Works is the old post office, now the Clydesdale Bank; and in the distance the twin spires of the Catholic Church. The origin of the name, Steelyard, is a matter of speculation. Many people think that a steel yard measure was fixed to a wall here, where weavers could bring their cloth to be measured. However, the name does not appear in the records until the weaving trade was almost extinct in Bathgate. It seems more likely that the name derives from the presence of a 'steelyard' – a weighing machine worked by a balance, where farmers and traders could weigh their loads, or travellers on the turnpike have their loads weighed, as their tolls were charged by weight. After they moved from the Burgh Muir, Bathgate's fairs were held here – feeing fairs where agricultural workers were hired.

Boghead House was the eighteenth century mansion house at the centre of the estate of the Durham family. In the late eighteenth century a daughter inherited and it was during the lairdship of her son, Thomas Durham Weir, that a seam of coal was found on the estate and was leased to Russel and Sons, the Falkirk coalmasters. For their miners, Russel built rows of cottages which were named Durhamtown, after the laird. As they were built during the Crimean War, each row was named after a battle or a general: Inkerman, Balaklava, Cardigan, etc. Durhamtown was briefly known as Kalafat after another incident in the war; the name later evolved into Kellyflat because of the high proportion of Irish living there. In 1851 James Young discovered that the Boghead coal was rich in mineral oil. To exploit this, he built the Bathgate Chemical Works. When the Boghead coal ran out, Young switched to shale for his oil works. The Durham family sold Boghead in 1929 and the house was demolished in 1962. The Falside housing scheme is built on part of the estate.

The National Strike of 1926 lives on in folk memory, but there was an equally serious national miners' strike in 1921, which lasted from April to July and caused great hardship and bitterness. By the third week of the strike, the *Courier* reported that 'A force estimated at 1,000, of marines and soldiers are stationed in West Lothian. All the pits have armed guards. The chief centres for the armed force are Bathgate, Bo'ness and Linlithgow'. The duty of the soldiers was 'to ensure that men employed in pumping are not molested by irresponsible persons'. At first it was naval ratings who guarded Bathgate pits, but in early May they were replaced by men of the Royal Scots. The government sent in troops to keep order and because the mine owners feared that the miners would try to damage the pits by preventing pumping. Then the pits would flood, causing more expense to the owners and so putting more pressure on them to settle. Boghead Pit (pictured here) was one of the three pits owned by Gavin Paul & Sons, whose miners were housed in the Paulville Rows. Boghead Colliery was just south of the North British Steel Foundry.

BATHGATE FROM NORTH

B 8319

Despite the caption, this is really a view from the east; taken from above Glenmavis Drive and looking east across Glenmavis Bowling Green and the High Church towards Easton Bing. Easton Colliery was the last and the largest of Bathgate's coal mines. Sunk by the Balbardie Coal Company in 1896-98 and taken over by William Baird & Co. in 1907, it was one of the most successful of West Lothian pits. It was connected below ground with Balbardie Pit, which functioned as a training mine and an escape route from Easton. Easton was notorious for roof falls, and its worst accident occurred in 1954, when three miners were killed – William Love, Thomas McLean and William Tracey. In 1966 the National Coal Board declared Easton to have a future of at least 15 to 20 years. However, it closed in 1973, throwing 400 men out of work and bringing to an end over 300 years of coal mining around Bathgate.

The buildings on the left hand side of High Hopetoun Street have all gone – demolished because of the subsidence of old mine workings. Those on the right have been more fortunate. The sandstone tenement on the corner survives, as does the building with the turret – highlighted by an arrow on the postcard. From 1895 to 1914 this was Bathgate's Post Office, with the postmaster's house on the upper storey. It was designed by Captain Speirs of Bathgate, in imitation of Coatbridge Post Office. The eighteenth century houses up the hill from it were knocked down and replaced by the present library which, though much in need of more space, is restricted to a single storey because of under-mining on the site. In January 1976 cracks appeared in shops and offices in High Hopetoun Street, doors jammed and plaster and masonry fell from buildings. The District Council applied for an emergency demolition order and sought compensation from the National Coal Board.

Until the opening of the Bathgate-Airdrie turnpike road (the Laigh or low road) in the mid 1790s, it was by Drumcross Hill that the Edinburgh road left Bathgate, heading up to the old high road to Bangour and Uphall. There was no link between Drumcross Road and the Torphichen road until the development of Torphichen Street. Proposals for it were first made as early as 1893, but it was not begun until 1903, and developed more rapidly after 1905 with the building of the Public School (now Balbardie Primary School). William Russell, the owner of the Corn Exchange, sold some land and donated some more to the Town Council so that the opening could be made from Torphichen Street into Drumcross Road.

This classic view of the High Street c.1910 shows what a handsome street was lost by the demolition and redevelopment of the late 1960s. The broad sweep of the High Street led down to the start of Main Street at the High Church and to the old town of Bathgate. The present High Church is the successor to the original parish church of Bathgate at Kirkton. In the seventeenth century the old church was abandoned in favour of a new building at the foot of Hill Street and North Street. This in turn was replaced by a church on the present site in 1739, which was replaced by the present church in 1884. The clock in the tower of the new church was given to Bathgate by former Provost John Waddell. West Lothian Council is now responsible for the 'town clock'. In the far distance can be seen the twin spires of the Catholic Church, St Mary's.

The Catholic Church began to revive in Bathgate with the coming of Irish workers to the mines, foundries and chemical works of Bathgate. Many Irish were also among the navvies who built the Bathgate railway in the late 1840s, some of whom settled in the town. The first Catholic church opened in 1858 in the former United Presbyterian church in Livery Street. By the end of the nineteenth century, the church was too small for the flourishing congregation. Fund-raising began and on 21 May 1907 the foundation stone of the new church on the site of the old was laid by the Archbishop of St Andrews and Edinburgh. It was a great day for Catholics and non-Catholics alike. A procession of 500 schoolchildren, representatives of the Irish societies in the town and Bathgate Public Band led the Archbishop and other clergy in an open carriage from the railway station to the church, through streets lined with crowds and decorated with banners, bunting, and an arch in Livery Street. And, of course, it rained.

Mill Road led to the Bathgate Mill, part of which was later incorporated into the Chieftain Forge. Bathgate Mill (a grain mill) was in existence certainly by 1768, but may be much older. It was powered by water drawn from the nearby Bathgate Water, which was stored in a millpond a few yards south of the mill. The long row of cottages in the distance, though fairly new when this photograph was taken in the early 1900s, are already showing signs of the subsidence that has since pulled them into strange angles and curves. The women on the right show two forms of baby transport – the middle-class child in a perambulator and the working-class child tucked into a plaid tied round her mother's body.

Many a Bathgate bairn learned to swim in the Mill Dam – most of them without the benefit of bathing costumes! The Mill Dam was the mill pond for Bathgate Mill where the water was stored up to power the mill wheel. After a fire the corn mill closed and was converted into an engineering workshop, then into Waite's spade and shovel manufactory (later the Chieftain Forge). In the background of the photograph can be seen cottages in Burnside Road (Cochrane Street at that time) and, beyond them, the tall chimneys of the Hopetoun Steel Works (better known as Renton and Fisher's). James Renton and John Fisher were both former employees of Dickson and Mann's foundry in Armadale, who set up their own foundry in 1899. By 1923 their foundry employed 310 men and took on some 30 apprentices a year. After the First World War, the firm specialised in the manufacture of coal-cutting machine castings, but the post-Second World War decline in heavy industries led to the firm going into receivership in 1979. It was taken over and staggered on until final closure in 1982.

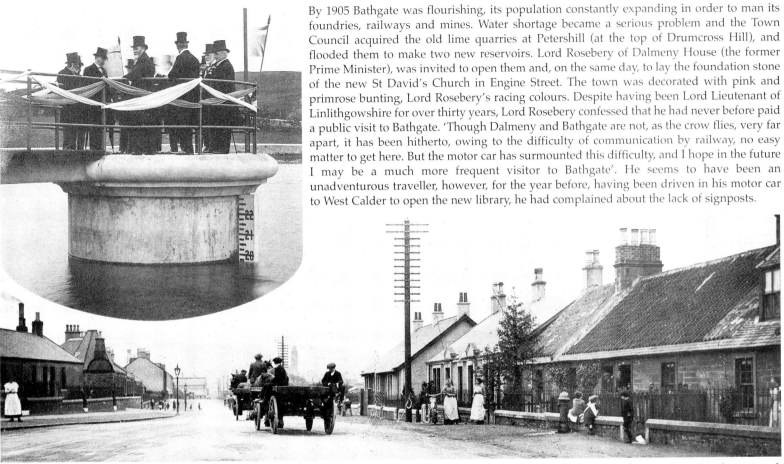

By 1905 Bathgate was flourishing, its population constantly expanding in order to man its foundries, railways and mines. Water shortage became a serious problem and the Town Council acquired the old lime quarries at Petershill (at the top of Drumcross Hill), and flooded them to make two new reservoirs. Lord Rosebery of Dalmeny House (the former Prime Minister), was invited to open them and, on the same day, to lay the foundation stone of the new St David's Church in Engine Street. The town was decorated with pink and primrose bunting, Lord Rosebery's racing colours. Despite having been Lord Lieutenant of Linlithgowshire for over thirty years, Lord Rosebery confessed that he had never before paid a public visit to Bathgate. 'Though Dalmeny and Bathgate are not, as the crow flies, very far apart, it has been hitherto, owing to the difficulty of communication by railway, no easy matter to get here. But the motor car has surmounted this difficulty, and I hope in the future I may be a much more frequent visitor to Bathgate'. He seems to have been an unadventurous traveller, however, for the year before, having been driven in his motor car to West Calder to open the new library, he had complained about the lack of signposts.

Bridgend was the hamlet at the far side of the bridge which carried the Glasgow road over the Bathgate Water, or Bog Burn – the boundary of Bathgate burgh at this point. Bridgend came under West Lothian County Council and had its own school - Bridgend Infant School, better known as the Wee Mair (or Muir, from Bathgate Muir). This view looks east towards Bathgate, with the distinctive house at the foot of Muir Road visible on the left. By the 1920s Bathgate Burgh was bursting at the seams and new council houses were needed to solve the town's chronic housing problems. In 1930 Bridgend and Kirkton were incorporated into the burgh, increasing the burgh's population from 9,000 to 11,000 and making much more land available for house-building.

In 1909 the *Courier* reported, 'a severe earthquake shock was felt at Bridgend, Bathgate, which caused considerable alarm. No serious damage was done, but the people in their houses got a severe shaking, being thrown here and there, while dishes were rattled all over the shelves.'

In 1914 the post office moved from High Hopetoun Street to a fine new building in the Steelyard, probably the finest in the town centre. The *Courier* described the various departments: the 'telegraphist department, and… the messengers' room, where the young lads are waiting ready to dash off with a "wire" a few seconds after it has been received…' The telephone room 'is a place of wonder to the man in the street. A call is made from Bathgate to London, Glasgow, Edinburgh, and, hey presto, within a few minutes, if the wires are clear, we are conversing with some one many miles away as easily as if he was at our side'. In 1977 the post office moved to a new site in South Bridge Street, and three years later, the old building became the Clydesdale Bank. Next door to it was the Buttercup Dairy Company, and on the left of the photograph can be seen the McLagan Fountain given to Bathgate by the wife of the local MP, to mark the opening of the Bathgate water works. Silhouetted against the sky is the distinctive Italianate tower of St David's Church.

George Street was made a pedestrian precinct in 1977 and, despite the fears of shop-keepers at the time, it remains the main shopping street. Bathgate was substantially changed in the late 1960s as part of the 'Comprehensive Re-development' of the town. Much needed to be done to clear away the detritus of the heavy engineering and coal mining industries, as they gave way to a new era of truck manufacturing and electronics. Many residents still lived in old sub-standard properties, but renovation rather than demolition would have saved many fine seventeenth and eighteenth century houses. The redevelopment was so 'comprehensive' that most of the old town has been lost: Hill Street, North Street, Market Street, the Bunker (Brown Square), and most of Main Street and the High Street have all disappeared. The destruction was done with the best of intentions, but it was a sad loss to Bathgate.

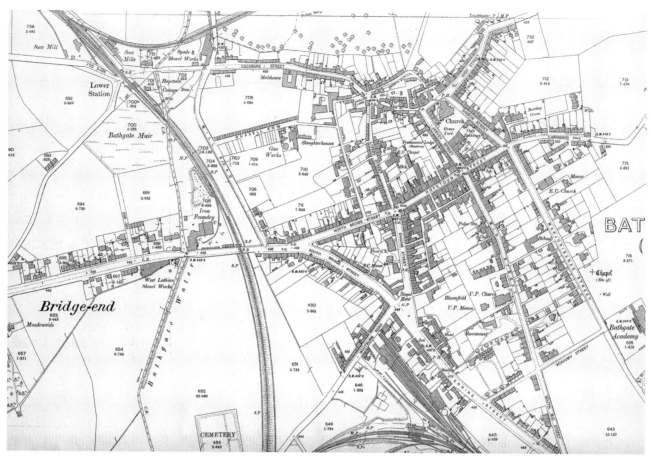

Bathgate in 1897. The old town can be seen grouped along the main roads – the Torphichen Road, High Street, Main Street and Cochrane Street. Compare its haphazard layout to the 'New Town' of Bathgate laid out on a grid pattern like Edinburgh's New Town: Gideon, Jarvey, Livery, Hopetoun, Marjoribanks and Mid Streets. 'The old town', noted the Imperial Gazetteer in the mid 1850s, 'is built on a steep ridge and the streets are narrow and crooked. The new town is built on a regular plan, and has a good appearance. Within these few years, the town has been considerably extended. Many good private houses have been built, and some large public buildings such as the academy, the gas work, a distillery and a brewery, are recent. Much additional stir has been created in the place by the opening of the railways, and by the commencement of the Boghead coal mines'. At this date there was no Union Road, which was built in the 1920s to provide a more direct route to the railway station from Mid and Marjoribanks Streets. Bathgate grew rapidly thereafter with the building of major new council housing schemes.

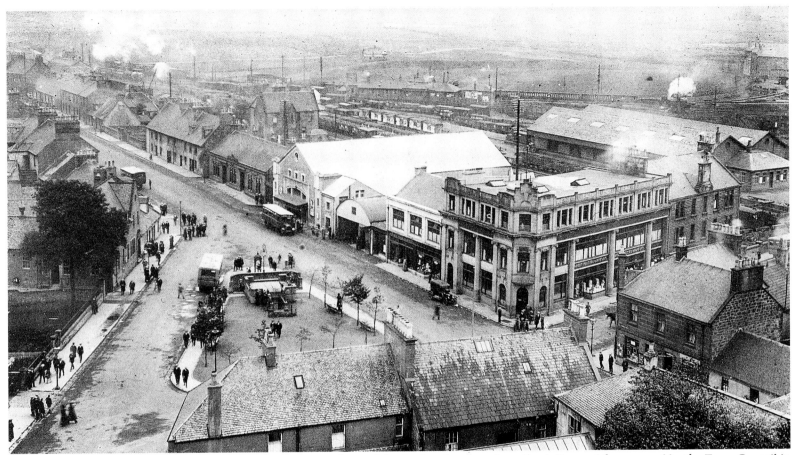

This view from St David's Church tower shows the triangular shape of the Steelyard and confirms the daftness of the proposal by the Town Council in the 1930s to re-name it George Circus. The Council eventually settled for George Place, but it is seldom known as anything other than the Steelyard. On the corner of Whitburn Road stand the Emporium buildings (designed and built by T.K. Irvine, architect, builder and Bathgate Provost) and opened in 1916 as offices for the Prudential Insurance Company, then gradually taken over by Greig's electrical and furniture business. Grieg's store closed in 1981.

The light-roofed building to the left of Greig's was Green's Pavilion, a cinema whose entrance hall was built of Caen stone and terrazzo mosaic work, with a floral and leaf design ceiling. Though now a Bingo Hall, the interior is a fine example of the cinema design of its period. In the distance can be seen the extensive railway yards.

In 1932 the name Engine Street fell into disfavour with the Town Council and Provost Wright complained that outsiders mocked Bathgate for calling one of its main streets by so prosaic a name. Bailie MacRae agreed: 'an engine had no music about it. It was as suggestive of music as flinging bricks into a wagon'. So, in order to sound more 'euphonious', Engine Street as far as the Steelyard became George Street (named after King George V) and the Steelyard became George Place. The part of the street shown here became King Street. Beyond Green's Pavilion on the right can be seen the Bathgate Inn, dating from c. 1800 and one of the oldest pubs in Bathgate. It has been replaced by a pub called the Engine Room, a name which neatly encapsulates reminders of the old name of the street, the steam engine of the early coal mines and the many steam locomotives which used to operate on the railways lines behind the pub during the heyday of Bathgate's railway age. On the other side of the road the Commercial, another pub with a long history, still survives as the Central Point.

Clinkin Stane steading and cottages stood on the south side of the old road to Bangour, 300 yards beyond the road up to the Knock. Sylvester Sprightly wrote in the *Courier* in 1877 that 'The stone known as the Clinking Stone stood beside the old steading, but was broken up and removed by a former tenant more than forty years ago. It was nothing more nor less than a large whin boulder, but had a clear chink like a bell when struck with a hammer'. The road up to the Knock was once known as the Salters' Road. It got the name, Sylvester Sprightly tells us, 'as being the regular thoroughfare for carriers and others who were conveying salt, in former times a valuable commodity… from Bo'ness salt pans to Bathgate and the south'.

This postcard was captioned 'Bathgate's new estate': i.e. Ravencraigs (or The Craigs), on which farm Clinkin Stane cottages stood. The Craigs was bought by Bathgate Town Council in 1907 in order to get access to the valuable water rights. 'There are a number of wells on the Craigs Farm,' the *Courier* reported, 'and the sources of supply are so situated that they can be conveniently diverted into the existing water-shed…Whinstone abounds on the grounds, and may also prove a valuable asset to the burgh… The Craigs is a good arable and dairy farm, extending to 140 acres (of which about 18 acres are plantation)'. A few years ago Ravencraigs was opened to the public as a small country park, where the remains of the old farmhouse can be seen.

The Knock lies about a mile north-east of the town on the edge of the Bathgate Hills. Until 1975 West Lothian claimed to be the Scottish county with the lowest highest point – the Knock (1,000 feet). Since local government re-organisation West Lothian's highest point has been West Cairn Hill in the Pentlands (1,845 feet). In 1936 Colonel Sutherland, member of a prominent Bathgate family, gave the Knock to the people of Bathgate... 'For some time I have been looking around for something which I might hand over to my native town as a small memorial to my late parents and brother; something which would be appreciated by the inhabitants of Bathgate... The Knock has locally, a considerable sentimental value, and perhaps affords one of the finest views... Mrs Sutherland and I would be prepared to hand over to the town free of all cost this piece of ground, making access to the Knock Hill a public right instead of a privilege as a present... if the Town Council... agree to keep it in order in its natural condition for all time to come'.

The pall of smoke which lies over Bathgate is a reminder of the heavy industry which brought prosperity to the few and toil to the many. Tall chimneys mark the sites of coal mines, the North British Steel Foundry, Renton and Fisher's Foundry and Wolfe's Shovel Works. This is Bathgate from Balbardie Road, showing the Bathgate Bowling Club's green, and beyond it, the rear of some of the houses in Marjoribanks Street. Bathgate's prospering middle-class families built some fine villas in this area in the late nineteenth century, including Wellpark (left, beyond bowling green), built by Dr Longmuir. Bathgate Bowling Green opened in 1915 and was often known as the 'high' green – partly because of its location and partly perhaps because of its reputation for being 'toffee-nosed'. At its opening Dan Robertson (the president) said that 'Although the green had been put down in an aristocratic quarter of town, it must not be supposed that it was put there for the purpose of catering for those aristocrats'.

OPENING OF BATHGATE EXTENDED GOLF COURSE
DRIVING THE FIRST BALL

At Bathgate Golf Club in May 1905, the *Courier* reported, 'in the presence of a large and fashionable gathering, the opening of the extended course to 18 holes was performed… As the people assembled at the Golf House in the morning, the ladies being attired in bright and pretty costumes, the scene, which resembled a garden party in no small degree, was of an attractive and picturesque character… Dr Kirk presented Mr John MacNab Jr, club president [and owner of Glenmavis Distillery] with a silver mounted club suitably inscribed in recognition of the great interest he has manifested in the Golf Club. Mr MacNab, in accepting the club, briefly returned thanks and drove off the first ball with the club amidst loud cheers, the drive being a particularly fine one… At the close of the foursome, on the invitation of the president, a large company were entertained to lunch. After a recherché repast, a short toast list was disposed of. '

The Liberator Lodge No. 475 was a friendly society, a branch of the International Order of Good Templars. Friendly societies became hugely popular in the nineteenth century, and grew out of small local societies set up to provide sickness benefits and funeral expenses. These small societies were financially unviable, so national societies were formed in the nineteenth century with the financial resources to remain solvent. The Good Templars was one of these national friendly societies; it was a temperance organisation and was unusual in admitting women. Other large societies with branches in Bathgate were the Shepherds, Gardeners, Foresters, Hibernians and the Rechabites. The friendly societies appealed to the better-off working class, those who could afford the small weekly payments and who prized their respectability. As well as financial security, the friendly societies offered the regalia and secret mysteries copied from freemasonry and the fellowship of social events and processions. In 1909 one in four of the population of Bathgate was a friendly society member. The coming of the welfare state in 1948 killed off most of them, by removing the need for the insurance they provided.

DOCTRINA SED,
VIM PROMOVET INSITAM
The FLAG of
OUR TEACHERS
MAY THE MARCH OF
PROGRESS
JOHN NEWLANDS ESQ.
Late of JAMAICA,
FOUNDER & ENDOWER
of the
BATHGATE ACADEMY
BORN APRIL
WHILE GENEROUS ACTIONS,
IN HONOUR
OF
BATHGATE ACADEMY
TRUSTEES

The Newland's Memorial Choir was set up to raise funds to erect a memorial to John Newland whose money was bequeathed for the founding of a free school for Bathgate bairns – Bathgate Academy. As early as the 1850s it was intended to create a memorial to be placed in the two niches on the front of the Academy. After the serious fire of 1906 one of the niches was replaced by a window, so the Town Council was asked to find another site for the memorial and settled on the Steelyard. Fundraising began under the energetic leadership of Parish Councillor Charles Campbell and a design was commissioned from Professor Percy Portsmouth. A model of his design was displayed in the Royal Scottish Academy on the Mound in 1910, a bronze warrior of Light and Learning triumphing over Darkness and Ignorance, which, mounted on its base, would have been 16 feet high. Between 1903 and 1911 the Memorial Choir held open-air concerts in fields behind Glenmavis Distillery, attracting audiences of over 1,000, but nevertheless the project foundered and it was not until 2000 that a more modest memorial was raised to John Newland in Main Street.

The 1st Bathgate Boys' Brigade Company was set up in Bathgate Parish (High) Church Hall in February 1897. One hundred boys enrolled in the first year and the brigade flourished, holding annual sports days and even a BB gala day. By 1908 the 120 boys could not all be drilled in the one hall and a second hall was needed. In 1911 the company was one of the largest in Scotland and its annual concert and 'assault-at-arms' entirely filled the Corn Exchange. Addressing the huge audience, the Provost was sure that none of the Boys' Brigade were responsible for any of the 'deplorable practices' then troubling the town: 'chalk-marking of buildings and the throwing of orange peel on the pavements'. A 2nd company was set up in 1961 for boys in the huge new housing scheme at Boghall and since then 3rd and 4th companies have also been set up. This photograph shows the 1st company, probably in the 1950s or 1960s, before the pill-box hat was abandoned in favour of the glengarry. The 1st company celebrated its centenary in 1997 and continues to flourish.

The Coronation of King George V in 1911 was marked in Bathgate by a day of festivities: an open-air church service at Balbardie House followed by sports, a procession of 3,000 children stretching for a mile through the decorated streets, a treat consisting of beef and potatoes, tea, cakes and fruit served to 200 poor people at the Picturedrome and a banquet given by the Provost and Town Council for 150 gentlemen in the Corn Exchange. 'At the conclusion of the banquet,' reported the *Courier*, 'the company formed in procession and accompanied by two bands and a huge concourse of townspeople, marched to the site of the bonfire opposite the Knock Hill. About 10.45, the huge cone-shaped pile, which had taken many weeks to construct and which was over 45 feet in height, was lighted by Miss Robertson, daughter of the Provost... It is estimated that about 5,000 people were in the vicinity of the bonfire... many of the young people engaging in dancing...'

Kirkton Public Park was built by Bathgate Town Council in the early 1920s with the help of a government scheme to create work for the unemployed. Some 75% of the men who worked on it were unemployed Great War ex-servicemen. The park was built on an eighteen-acre field – Lodge Park – part of the old Kirkton estate. Kirkton House (built in 1599) was demolished in 1862; its stone was used to build 81 and 83 Mid Street, but its Gothic arched gateway still survives at the entrance to the park. The park was opened on 25 June 1927 by the Secretary of State for Scotland and featured a putting green, a pond with a rustic bridge, swings, roundabouts, a statue of Burns and Highland Mary (complete with heads and hands!) and the bandstand – a concrete shell which reflected the sound back to the audience. Over the years the bandstand held brass and pipe band concerts and (latterly) rock gigs. It has since been demolished.

When Kirkton Public Park was created in 1924, hundreds of cedar, larch and hardwood trees were planted. The road in the foreground is Puir Wife's Brae. Many theories have been put forward as to the origin of the name, but it is not known with any certainty. In 1901 the *Courier* printed a long tale claiming that the puir wife was Sister Agatha, who, disappointed in love, entered a monastery (sic) at Kirkton. There is no evidence at all for the existence of either Sister Agatha or the monastery. Puir Wife's Brae was long a favourite walk for Bathgate folk making a circuit out by the Kirk Roads and home by Drumcross Road. Writing in the *Courier*, James Forrest said that Puir Wife's Brae 'may be said to form the south-east spur of that range of elevated lands which, commencing at Ravencraig, run through the estates of Craigs, Drumcross, Limefield and Kirkton Mains... A little to the northward of the Puir Wife's Brae stands a clump of trees on a rising ground which for hundreds of years has been called the Warlock Hill'. Other local names which have been lost are the Craw Plantin' and Fairy Knowe – plantations to the north and west of the Brae.

Bathgate Lower Station was opened in 1856 by the Monkland Railway Company, on a new line connecting Bathgate with Blackston Junction on the Slamannan line, and thence with Bo'ness. The line was built, not into the centre of Bathgate, but to the west of the town, in order to serve the Boghead mineral fields which at that time were producing the famous Torbanite coal. Much of this coal was used by James Young to produce mineral oil at his Bathgate Chemical Works, but there was also a lucrative market for it in England which Russel & Sons, the coalmasters, were determined to exploit; their Torbanite would be sent by the new line to Bo'ness for shipment. The new railway required the building of the fine twelve-arch viaduct over the River Avon at Westfield, and it joined the Wilsontown, Morningside and Coltness Railway (via Whitburn and Fauldhouse to Wishaw) at Boghead. The Lower Station closed to passengers in 1930 and to goods trains in 1963.

Bathgate Upper Station c. 1970. Bathgate was an important centre of the railway network and had two stations: the Upper off Whitburn Road and the Lower at Bridgend. The Lower served lines to the north and the south-west, while the Upper served the Edinburgh line. However, travellers from Edinburgh wanting to travel on to the west had to walk the half-mile from the Upper to the Lower Station for the onward journey. When the Bathgate-Coatbridge line opened in 1863, a connecting loop was created to the Bathgate-Edinburgh line, so through travel became possible. The original Bathgate station (on the site of the present one) was replaced by a new Upper Station on the connecting loop. Bathgate Upper closed to passengers in 1956, but continued to carry freight particularly to the huge BMC/British Leyland plant at Bathgate. The line re-opened to passengers in 1986 and has become one of the busiest in Scotland, helping to regenerate West Lothians economy and its housing market. Plans are afoot to re-open the railway line west to Airdrie.

Bathgate Upper Station, looking west. The class system operated even in railway travel, for by 1897 the Upper Station boasted separate first, second and third class waiting rooms for ladies, and first and second class for men. In 1896 an average of 90 passengers passed through the station daily, a total which increased the following year when a loop was constructed between Bathgate Lower and Upper Stations. In 1913 the platform had to be raised following complaints from women: 'In these days of tight-fitting skirts, this difficulty of comfortably getting into or from a carriage has been positively dangerous to ladies.' The *Courier* also called for a second footbridge to ease passenger congestion: 'Every Saturday it is quite a common sight to see several panting men and women fighting their way among a crowd on top of the bridge.' With the prevalence of coal mining in West Lothian, Bathgate became the hub of coal transport, serving in its heyday some 40 pits, with over 50 locomotives (mainly goods engines) in its engine sheds.